From Chandoha, *Six Puppies Postcards*, a Dover Publication

From Chandoha, *Six Puppies Postcards*, a Dover Publication

From Chandoha, *Six Puppies Postcards*, a Dover Publication

From Chandoha, *Six Puppies Postcards*, a Dover Publication

From Chandoha, *Six Puppies Postcards*, a Dover Publication

From Chandoha, *Six Puppies Postcards*, a Dover Publication